Merry Christmas
to
Drew
with love from
Grandaddy and
Grandmama - 2014

VOLCANO WAKES UP!

LISA WESTBERG PETERS

ILLUSTRATED BY
STEVE JENKINS

Henry Holt and Company • New York

VOLCANO

I'm the baby.

I'm much smaller than my

big sister volcanoes. I'm a little sleepy

now, but when I wake up, *watch out!* I throw

nasty tantrums. It always works—I get the most attention!

FERNS

We ferns love cool,
we ferns love
gray,
we ferns love
the mornings when
Fire-maker
sleeps
late. Let's
celebrate! Let's
uncurl
our
fiddleheads,
let's strrrrrretch out
our fronds,
let's
hang misty
streamers and throw
raindrops around.
Hey,
everyone,
come to the caldera.
Let's party!

LAVA FLOW CRICKET 1

Hey, bro, where R U?
I know it's early a.m.
:-< But I have a feeling
the Big V's gonna
shake tonite. The wind
is gonna blow & the
lava is gonna flow.
C U L8R. Call me!

ON THIS **ACTIVE VOLCANO** I PROCEED WITH **CAUTION**

SMALL BLACK ROAD

I
BUCKLE UP
FOR SAFETY
BUT I DON'T EXPECT TO
HAVE A
NICE DAY
FOR
EARTH CRACKS
I DIP,
FOR
STEEP CLIFFS
I TURN

SUN TO MOON

Moon, my friend! You look so pale.

Or is it just my glare? You should

Rest and dream for now, but why

Not meet me later over bread?

I'll ask the earth, my baker friend, at

Noon to bake you something warm.

Good morning, Moon! I'll see you tonight.

VOLCANO

Hey! It's a little
quiet around here.
It's time to kick up a lot of
dust and ash, time to shake the ground
and make a big stink. *Watch this, everybody!*

FERNS

Fire-maker's awake!
She's about to
make
this caldera
a lake of fire and
lava. Ah, the
party
must be over.
Put away all the
streamers.
Say
good-bye,
honeycreepers.
But wait . . . it's
not
hot yet. It's
not even warm
yet. What a
lucky
delay on this
beautiful day. Hey,
everybody, let's
party!

LAVA FLOW CRICKET 2

Hey, bro, I M way back in the cave. I was ZZZZZZ hard, but that nsty smll woke me up. P U! :-o The Big V must be cranking up. Where R U? Bye4now.

I SEE
A
CONSTRUCTION
ZONE
AHEAD

DARN!
THIS
ACTIVE
VOLCANO
IS
ALWAYS
UNDER
CONSTRUCTION

SMALL BLACK ROAD

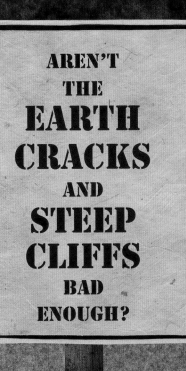

SUN

My baker friend has just begun!

I know because it's noon. I look straight

Down and see the steam escape her

Door. By twilight, she'll be finished

And Moon and I will share a feast.

Yes, the bread will be delicious.

VOLCANO

Look at me!
I can fling cinders
and ash into the sky. I can
huff and chuff and pour rivers of
lava down my side. *Rain, you can't douse my
fire. Wind, you can't blow it out. Fog, you can't hide it.*

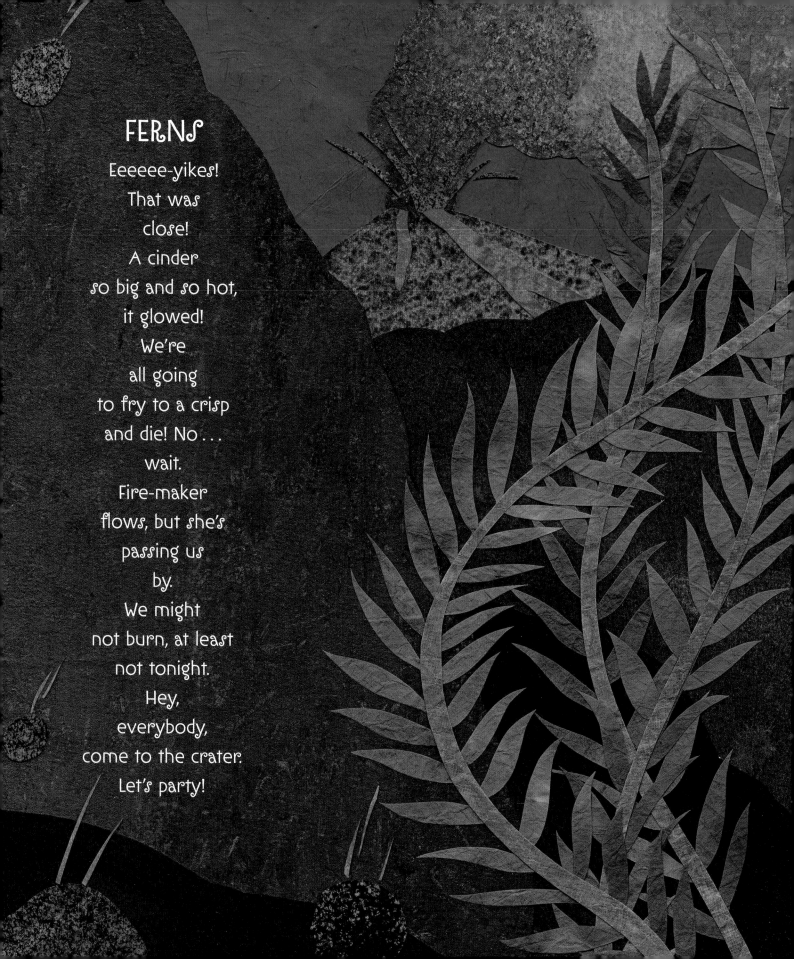

FERNS

Eeeeee-yikes!
That was
close!
A cinder
so big and so hot,
it glowed!
We're
all going
to fry to a crisp
and die! No...
wait.
Fire-maker
flows, but she's
passing us
by.
We might
not burn, at least
not tonight.
Hey,
everybody,
come to the crater.
Let's party!

LAVA FLOW CRICKET 1

Hey, bro, I M at the
AllUCanEat, AllNt,
HotLavaBBQ! The
food is xlnt—loads
of bugs toastd &
roastd by the heat!
:-) There U R. Look
up. Sweet, no?

OH NO!
THIS RED HOT
PAVING
OPERATION
IS GIVING
ME A
SOFT
SHOULDER
AND MELTING MY
FRESH
PAINT
SMALL BLACK ROAD

I'LL HAVE TO COME AGAIN!
HEY, THIS DETOUR IS A GREAT SCENIC ROUTE
I NEED TO DETOUR PAST SPATTER RAMPARTS AND STEAM VENTS

MOON TO SUN

Tonight, my sunny friend,

We haven't too much time.

I crack the oven door and . . .

Look! The bread is done.

It's hot and holds the oven's

Glow. Let's have a bite! I

Hope you dream tonight and

Thanks, my friend. I'm full.

VOLCANO

Moon, are you
already here? I should
go to bed, but I'm wide awake
and I'm bigger! I have new layers of
lava and cinders. *Sea, are you awake too?*
What should we do? I know! I'll send you a ribbon
of red lava,
a gift!
Moon,
watch
this!

lava lava lava lava lava lava

VOLCANO

The poems in *Volcano Wakes Up!* describe a day—from sunrise to moonrise—on an imaginary Hawaiian volcano. Volcanoes form the islands of the Hawaiian island chain, and all of them have their feet planted on the floor of the Pacific Ocean.

Most Hawaiian volcanoes are inactive, or dormant, but it's a different story on the Big Island of Hawai'i. The youngest (and smallest) volcano on the island is among the most active in the world. One of its older (and taller) volcano sisters is the biggest volcano in the world and also one of the most active.

Despite the hazards, millions of people safely visit Hawai'i Volcanoes National Park every year. They drive, walk, and bicycle on roads and trails that crisscross the park's two active volcanoes, Mauna Loa and Kilauea (pronounced KEY-low-WAY-uh).

Thousands of earthquakes shake the Big Island every year. Most of them are very small, but a few are large and can do damage. Some quakes are caused by molten rock moving along underground paths, and others occur when parts of the island shift.

People have always interpreted nature in different ways. Ancient Polynesians who settled the islands saw an erupting volcano as a living, angry goddess named Pele. They believed she erupted to destroy her enemies. The legends say that Pele originally came from Tahiti. The word comes from *kahiki* (kuh-HEE-kee) in the Hawaiian language, meaning "a foreign land." Pele searched for a home in the Hawaiian Islands and settled on Kilauea. Native Hawaiians today conduct religious ceremonies at a place they consider sacred, Kilauea caldera, the large crater at the summit of the volcano.

FERNS

After a volcano on the Big Island erupts, the new lava rock doesn't stay bare and lifeless for long. Native ferns and other plants start popping up very quickly in the volcano's moist cracks and crevices. One of these hardy plants is *hāpu'u pulu* (HAH-poo-oo poo-loo), a tree fern that grows only in Hawai'i.

Ferns grow in the rain forest near the summit of Kilauea. About a hundred inches of rain fall there each year. Hawai'i's native birds love the rain forest, but many species are endangered and hard to find. The 'apapane (uhh-puh-PUH-nay), a red honeycreeper, is common. It flits among the ferns and treetops and sips nectar from the red blossoms of the 'ōhi'a (oh-HEE-uh) tree.

LAVA FLOW CRICKETS

Lava-colored crickets live on the bare lava fields at low elevations where the climate is drier. Sometimes they move onto a lava flow only a month after it has cooled to solid rock. Lava flows exposed to the air start to form a hard crust almost immediately. If the flow is thin, it might cool to solid rock in a matter of days, but thick flows can take years to solidify.

The crickets rest during the day in protected lava cracks—many people never see them—and at night they come out to eat. They prefer to eat the insects that have been roasted to a crisp by the heat of an eruption!

SMALL BLACK ROAD

Lava flows and earthquakes damage the narrow, winding roads in the park. Although park managers try to rebuild roads, sometimes frequent eruptions make these efforts impossible.

Road and trail signs constantly remind visitors that they are traveling on active volcanoes: BEWARE OF EARTH CRACKS; SULPHUR BANK TRAIL; EARTHQUAKE TRAIL; VOLCANIC FUMES ARE HAZARDOUS TO YOUR HEALTH; FAULT ZONE: WATCH FOR CRACKS IN ROAD.

SUN AND MOON

Visitors and residents gather on the coast of the Big Island to see hot lava enter the ocean. The lava temperature is 2,200° Fahrenheit (1,204° Celsius), and when it hits seawater, it creates an enormous plume of steam, chemicals, and shattered lava.

The best time to watch this event is when the moon is full. A full moon always rises around the same time the sun sets. The hazy volcanic plume scatters the setting sun's fading light and turns the moon into an orange ball. What a visual feast in the middle of the Pacific Ocean—moonrise, sunset, and the warm glow of a volcano!

FOR MORE INFORMATION ABOUT HAWAI'I'S VOLCANOES, VISIT THE FOLLOWING WEB SITES:

Hawaiian Volcano Observatory [hvo.wr.usgs.gov];

Hawai'i Volcanoes National Park [www.nps.gov/havo].

AUTHOR'S NOTE

I was a tourist the first time I visited the Big Island of Hawai'i. But the island's active volcanoes brought me back over and over for extended stays. I've spent many weeks hiking, exploring, taking notes, and shooting photos on Kilauea Volcano. Everything about it fascinates me—the steam coming out of cracks in the ground, the glow of incandescent lava, the feel of black sand that was hot lava just hours earlier. I sat in on university geology classes, hovered over the volcano's active vent in a helicopter, and felt my first earthquake. Many people cheerfully answered my questions or otherwise helped me, but I would especially like to thank Jim and Audrey Wilson, Ted Pirsig and Val Crawford, Jim Anderson of the University of Hawai'i at Hilo, the tireless members of my writing group, and Dave, my traveling companion.

For Hawai'i Volcanoes National Park, an astonishing place
—L. W. P.

For Jamie
—S. J.

Henry Holt and Company, LLC, *Publishers since 1866*
175 Fifth Avenue, New York, New York 10010
www.HenryHoltKids.com

Henry Holt® is a registered trademark of Henry Holt and Company, LLC.
Text copyright © 2010 by Lisa Westberg Peters
Illustrations copyright © 2010 by Steve Jenkins
All rights reserved.
Distributed in Canada by H. B. Fenn and Company Ltd.

Library of Congress Cataloging-in-Publication Data
Peters, Lisa Westberg.
Volcano wakes up! / Lisa Westberg Peters ; illustrated by Steve Jenkins.—1st ed.
p. cm.
ISBN 978-0-8050-8287-6
1. Volcanoes—Juvenile poetry. 2. Children's poetry, American.
I. Jenkins, Steve, ill. II. Title.
PS3566.E75573V65 2009   811'.54—dc22   2008038225

First Edition—2010
The artist used cut-paper collage to create the illustrations for this book.
Printed in October 2009 in China by Leo Paper, Heshan City, Guangdong Province, on acid-free paper. ∞

1 3 5 7 9 10 8 6 4 2

A portion of the proceeds from this book will benefit the Hawai'i Natural History Association.